WordPress Design and Development
By
Jagdish Krishanlal Arora
techbagg@outlook.com

Table of Contents

Chapter 1: Introduction to WordPress

W hat is WordPress?

WordPress is an open-source content management system (CMS) and website-building platform. It's software that allows individuals and businesses to create and manage websites easily and efficiently. Some key characteristics of WordPress include:

User-Friendly: WordPress is known for its user-friendly interface, making it accessible to people with varying levels of technical expertise. You don't need to be a web developer to use it.

Customizability: You can customize the design and functionality of your website using themes and plugins. This allows you to create websites for a wide range of purposes, from blogs and business sites to e-commerce stores and portfolios.

Community and Support: WordPress has a large and active community of developers and users. This community provides support through forums, documentation, tutorials, and meetups, making it easier to get help and learn how to use WordPress effectively.

Scalability: WordPress is scalable, meaning it can handle websites of all sizes, from small personal blogs to large corporate websites with thousands of pages and high traffic.

SEO-Friendly: WordPress is designed with SEO (search engine optimization) in mind. There are many SEO plugins available that help improve your website's visibility on search engines.

Open Source: WordPress is open-source software, which means it's free to use, modify, and distribute. This open nature has led to its widespread adoption and continuous development.

2. Why Choose WordPress?

There are several reasons why you might choose WordPress for building your website:

Ease of Use: WordPress's intuitive interface allows beginners to get started quickly. You can easily add and edit content without needing extensive technical knowledge.

Customization: With thousands of themes and plugins available, you can create a website that perfectly matches your vision. Themes control the design, while plugins add functionality.

Community and Support: WordPress has a supportive community of users and developers. You can find answers to your questions, access tutorials, and even hire professionals for help.

Scalability: Whether you're starting small or planning a large website, WordPress can scale with your needs.

SEO Benefits: WordPress is inherently SEO-friendly, and you can further enhance its SEO capabilities with plugins like Yoast SEO.

Cost-Effective: The core WordPress software is free, and many themes and plugins are also free or reasonably priced. This can be cost-effective for businesses and individuals.

Security: WordPress takes security seriously and releases regular updates and patches to address vulnerabilities.

3. Understanding WordPress.org vs. WordPress.com

WordPress.org and WordPress.com are two different ways to use WordPress:

WordPress.org: This is where you can download the free, open-source WordPress software. You need to find a hosting provider, set up your domain, and install WordPress on your server. This option provides full control and flexibility but requires more technical know-how.

WordPress.com: This is a commercial platform that offers hosting and a simplified setup process. You can create a website on WordPress.com without worrying about hosting and server management. However, it has some limitations in terms of customization, and you may need to pay for certain features and a custom   domain.

Chapter 2: Domain and Hosting

Choosing a Domain Name: A domain name is your website's address on the internet. It's the web address people will use to find your site. Here are some tips for choosing a domain name:

Relevance: Your domain name should be relevant to the content or purpose of your website. It should give visitors an idea of what to expect.

Memorability: Pick a domain name that is easy to remember. Short, simple, and unique names are often best.

Avoid Special Characters and Numbers: Special characters and numbers can be confusing when spoken, so it's generally best to stick with letters.

Use Keywords: If possible, include keywords related to your website's topic or niche in your domain name. This can help with search engine optimization (SEO).

Consider Branding: If you're building a brand, use your brand name as the domain name. Consistency is key for branding.

Check Availability: Before finalizing your choice, check if the domain name is available. There are domain registrars (see below) that allow you to search for available domain names.

2. Selecting a Web Hosting Provider: Web hosting is a service that makes your website accessible on the internet. Here's how to choose a web hosting provider:

Type of Hosting: Decide what type of hosting you need. Shared hosting is cost-effective and suitable for small websites. VPS (Virtual Private Server) and dedicated hosting offer more resources and control but are pricier. Managed WordPress hosting is tailored for WordPress sites.

Reliability: Look for a hosting provider with a good track record of uptime (the time your site is online). Downtime can negatively impact your website's availability.

Speed: Website speed is crucial for user experience and SEO. Choose a hosting provider with fast servers and good performance.

Support: Ensure the hosting provider offers reliable customer support. You may need assistance with technical issues, so responsive support is essential.

Scalability: Consider your website's future growth. Choose a hosting provider that allows you to upgrade easily as your site's traffic and resource needs increase.

Security: Security is paramount. The hosting provider should offer features like SSL certificates, firewall protection, and regular backups.

Cost: Compare hosting plans and pricing. Some providers offer introductory discounts, so be sure to check renewal prices as well.

3. Registering Your Domain and Setting up Hosting:

Once you've chosen a domain name and a hosting provider, here are the steps to register your domain and set up hosting:

Domain Registration: If your hosting provider offers domain registration (many do), you can register your domain name during the hosting sign-up process. If not, you can use a separate domain registrar like GoDaddy, Namecheap, or Google Domains to register your domain.

Choose a Hosting Plan: Select the hosting plan that best suits your needs. This might be shared hosting, VPS hosting, or a managed WordPress hosting plan, depending on your website's requirements.

Complete the Purchase: Provide your contact and payment information to complete the purchase of your hosting plan and domain registration (if applicable).

DNS Configuration: Once you've registered your domain and purchased hosting, you'll need to configure your domain's DNS (Domain Name System) settings to point to your hosting provider's servers. Your hosting provider will provide you with the necessary DNS information.

Website Setup: After configuring DNS, you can start setting up your website. This typically involves installing a content management system (e.g., WordPress) and customizing your site's design and content.

Chapter 3: WordPress Installation

Installing WordPress is a fundamental step in setting up your website. You can choose between manual installation and one-click installation, depending on your preferences and hosting provider. Let's explore both options:

Manual Installation: Installing WordPress manually involves more steps and technical knowledge but provides greater control over the process. Here's how to do it:

Download WordPress: Visit the official WordPress website at https://wordpress.org/download/ and download the latest version of WordPress to your computer.

Upload WordPress Files: Using an FTP (File Transfer Protocol) client like FileZilla or your hosting provider's file manager, upload the downloaded WordPress files to your web server. You typically upload them to the root directory of your website (often called "public_html" or "www").

Create a Database: In your hosting control panel (usually cPanel or a similar platform), create a new MySQL database and a user with full privileges for that database. Make sure to note down the database name, username, and password.

Configure wp-config.php: Locate the wp-config-sample.php file in the WordPress files you uploaded earlier. Rename it to wp-config.php and edit it using a text editor. Enter your database details (database name, username, and password) where indicated.

Run the Installation: Open a web browser and navigate to your domain name. You should see the WordPress installation wizard. Follow the on-screen instructions, including setting up your site's title, admin username, and password.

Login to Your Dashboard: After completing the installation, you can access your WordPress dashboard by going to yourdomain.com/wp-admin. Log in using the username and password you set during installation.

One-Click Installation via Hosting: Many hosting providers offer one-click installation scripts (like Softaculous or Fantastico) that automate the process of installing WordPress. Here's how to do it:

Log in to Your Hosting Control Panel: Access your hosting control panel (often cPanel) using the credentials provided by your hosting provider.

Find the Auto-Installer: Look for an option like "Softaculous" or "Installatron." Click on it to open the auto-installer tool.

Select WordPress: In the auto-installer, find and select WordPress from the list of available applications.

Choose Installation Options: You will be prompted to configure your WordPress installation. This typically includes choosing the domain where you want to install WordPress, setting up an admin username and password, and selecting your preferred language.

Install: Click the "Install" button to begin the installation process. The auto-installer will handle the database creation and file setup for you.

Access Your Dashboard: Once the installation is complete, you will receive a confirmation message with links to your website and the WordPress admin login page. You can log in to your dashboard using the admin credentials you specified during installation.

Which Option to Choose: Manual Installation: This option provides more control and is useful if you're comfortable with server configurations. It's also beneficial if you want to install a specific version of WordPress or customize the installation process.

One-Click Installation: This is a quicker and more user-friendly option, making it suitable for beginners. It's especially convenient when your hosting provider offers this feature.

The choice ultimately depends on your level of technical expertise and preference. Both methods will result in a functional WordPress   website.

Chapter 4: Initial WordPress Setup

Accessing the WordPress dashboard, configuring basic settings, and choosing a WordPress theme are essential steps in setting up your WordPress website. Let's go through each of these steps:

1. Accessing the WordPress Dashboard: The WordPress dashboard is the backend or administrative area of your website, where you can create, edit, and manage content. To access it:

Open your web browser.

Enter your website's URL followed by "/wp-admin" (e.g., yourwebsite.com/wp-admin).

You'll see a login page. Enter the username and password you created during the WordPress installation.

After logging in, you'll be taken to the WordPress dashboard.

2. Configuring Basic Settings: Before you start creating content, it's essential to configure some basic settings for your website. Here's how:

General Settings: In the dashboard, go to "Settings" > "General."

Set the Site Title and Tagline: These will appear in search engine results and on your website.

Choose the WordPress Address (URL) and Site Address (URL): Ensure these are correct. Usually, they should match your domain name.

Set the Time zone and Date Format according to your location and preferences.

Click the "Save Changes" button.

Permalinks: In the dashboard, go to "Settings" > "Permalinks."

Choose a permalink structure for your website's URLs. The "Post Name" option is commonly used for SEO-friendly URLs.

Click the "Save Changes" button.

Reading Settings: In the dashboard, go to "Settings" > "Reading."

Determine whether you want your homepage to display your latest blog posts or a static page. If you choose a static page, select the pages for your homepage and blog page.

Click the "Save Changes" button.

Discussion Settings (Optional): In the dashboard, go to "Settings" > "Discussion."

Configure settings related to comments and discussions on your site. Adjust as needed, depending on your preferences.

Click the "Save Changes" button.

Media Settings: In the dashboard, go to "Settings" > "Media."

Adjust image sizes if necessary. The default settings are suitable for most websites.

Click the "Save Changes" button.

3. Choosing a WordPress Theme:

Selecting the right WordPress theme is crucial because it determines your site's appearance and layout. Here's how to choose and install a theme:

In the dashboard, go to "Appearance" > "Themes."

You'll see the "Themes" page, which displays the currently installed themes.

Click the "Add New" button at the top to browse and search for themes in the WordPress Theme Directory. You can use the search bar and filters to find themes that match your site's style and functionality.

When you find a theme you like, hover over it, and click the "Install" button. After installation, click the "Activate" button to make it your active theme.

To customize your theme further, go to "Appearance" > "Customize." Here, you can adjust settings related to colours, fonts, layout, and more, depending on the theme you've chosen.

If you have a premium theme purchased from a third-party source, you can upload it by going to "Appearance" > "Themes" > "Add New" > "Upload Theme."

Remember that you can change your theme at any time, so feel free to experiment until you find the one that best suits your website's needs and style.

Chapter 5: Understanding the WordPress Dashboard

Understanding the components of the WordPress dashboard and how to navigate it is essential for managing your website effectively. Here's an overview of the key dashboard components and how to navigate them:

1. Dashboard Components: The WordPress dashboard is organized into several main components and sections:

Admin Toolbar: This is located at the top of the screen and provides quick access to various administrative functions. You can access your profile, create new posts or pages, and access other settings from here.

Admin Menu: The left-hand sidebar contains the primary navigation menu for your WordPress dashboard. It includes links to essential areas such as Posts, Media, Pages, Comments, Appearance, Plugins, Users, Tools, and Settings. Depending on the plugins and themes you've installed, you may see additional menu items.

Main Content Area: This is the central area of the dashboard where you will see various widgets and information boxes. These widgets provide at-a-glance information about your site, including recent activity, draft posts, and more. You can customize this area by adding or removing widgets.

Quick Draft: In the main content area, there is a "Quick Draft" box where you can quickly create new draft posts or pages without navigating to a separate editor.

Activity: This section displays recent comments on your posts and any other activity related to your site.

At a Glance: Here, you can see an overview of your site's content, including the number of published posts, pages, and comments.

WordPress News: This widget provides the latest news and updates from the official WordPress blog. It's a great way to stay informed about the latest developments in the WordPress ecosystem.

2. Navigating the Dashboard: Navigating the WordPress dashboard is straightforward. Here's a step-by-step guide:

Log In: To access the dashboard, log in to your WordPress site by visiting your site's URL followed by "/wp-admin" (e.g., yourwebsite.com/wp-admin). Enter your username and password.

Admin Toolbar: Once logged in, you'll see the admin toolbar at the top of the screen. This toolbar provides quick access to various functions, including editing your profile, creating new content, viewing your site, and logging out.

Admin Menu: The left-hand sidebar contains the primary navigation menu. Click on any of the menu items to access different sections of your dashboard. For example, to create a new post, click "Posts" and then "Add New."

Sub-Menus: Some menu items have sub-menus that appear when you hover over them. These sub-menus provide access to specific functions or settings related to the main menu item.

Dashboard Widgets: The main content area of the dashboard contains widgets that provide information and shortcuts. You can rearrange or remove widgets by clicking on the "Screen Options" tab at the top-right corner of the screen.

Help Tab: If you ever need assistance while in the dashboard, click on the "Help" tab at the top-right corner. This provides context-sensitive help and links to official WordPress documentation.

User Profile: You can access and edit your user profile by clicking on your username in the admin toolbar. Here, you can change your password, set your display name, and manage other personal settings.

Log Out: To log out of the dashboard, click your username in the admin toolbar and select "Log Out."

Navigating the WordPress dashboard becomes more intuitive as you use it regularly. It's designed to be user-friendly, allowing you to manage your website's content and settings with ease.

Chapter 6: Creating Your First Post

Adding and formatting text, uploading images and media, and using categories and tags are fundamental tasks when creating content on a WordPress website. Let's explore each of these aspects:

1. Adding and Formatting Text:

To add and format text in a WordPress post or page:

Create a New Post or Page: In the WordPress dashboard, go to "Posts" > "Add New" for a new blog post or "Pages" > "Add New" for a new page.

Add Text: Click in the main content area and start typing your text. You can also copy and paste text from another source.

Text Formatting: Use the formatting toolbar above the text area to format your text. Common formatting options include:

Bold: Highlight text and click the "B" icon.

Italic: Highlight text and click the "I" icon.

Bullet and Numbered Lists: Create lists using the list icons.

Alignment: Align text left, centre, or right.

Heading Styles: Use headings (H1, H2, etc.) to structure your content. Choose the appropriate heading style from the dropdown.

Paragraph and Line Breaks: Press "Enter" for a new paragraph and "Shift + Enter" for a line break within the same paragraph.

Block Editor: If you're using the block editor (Gutenberg), you can use various content blocks for more advanced formatting, including headings, paragraphs, images, galleries, and more. Click the "+" icon to add a block.

Preview: Click the "Preview" button to see how your content will appear on the live site.

Save or Publish: When you're satisfied with your content, click "Save Draft" to save your work, or "Publish" to make it live on your website.

2. Uploading Images and Media: To upload images and media to your WordPress posts or pages:

Create or Edit a Post/Page: Open the post or page where you want to add media.

Insert Media: Click the "Add Media" button located above the text editor.

Upload Files: Click the "Upload Files" tab to upload new images or media from your computer. You can also select files that are already in your media library.

Select and Insert: After uploading, select the media you want to insert into your post or page. You can choose multiple items if needed.

Set Options: Configure image settings, such as alignment, size, and link behaviour, in the right-hand panel.

Insert into Post/Page: Click the "Insert into post" or "Insert into page" button to add the selected media to your content.

Preview and Publish: Preview your post or page to ensure the media appears as expected, then save or publish your content.

3. Categories and Tags: Categories and tags help organize and categorize your content, making it easier for visitors to find related posts. Here's how to use them:

Categories: Categories are broader topics or sections of your website. For example, if you run a food blog, you might have categories like "Recipes," "Restaurant Reviews," and "Cooking Tips."

To assign a category to a post, find the "Categories" box in the post editor, check the relevant category, or create a new one, and click "Add New Category."

Tags: Tags are more specific keywords or phrases that describe the content of a post in more detail. For a food blog post, tags could include "Italian Cuisine," "Pasta Recipes," and "Homemade Tomato Sauce."

To add tags, find the "Tags" box in the post editor, enter your tags separated by commas, and click "Add."

Using Categories and Tags: Properly using categories and tags helps with website organization and SEO. Visitors can click on a category or tag to view related content.

Widget and Navigation Menus: You can display categories and tags in widgets or navigation menus on your site, making it easier for users to explore your content by category or topic.

By adding and formatting text, uploading images and media, and effectively using categories and tags, you can create engaging and organized content that enhances the user experience on your WordPress   website.

Chapter 7: Creating Your First Page

Understanding the difference between posts and pages in WordPress and knowing how to create and organize them is crucial for effectively structuring your website. Let's explore these aspects:

1. Difference Between Posts and Pages:

Posts: Dynamic Content: Posts are typically used for dynamic, time-sensitive content, such as blog articles, news updates, or regular content updates.

Organized by Date: Posts are organized in reverse chronological order, with the most recent content appearing at the top. They are usually displayed on your site's blog page.

Categories and Tags: You can categorize and tag posts to organize them into specific topics or subjects, making it easier for readers to find related content.

Comments: Posts often allow and encourage comments and discussions.

RSS Feeds: Posts are included in RSS feeds, allowing readers to subscribe to your site's latest content.

Pages:

Static Content: Pages are typically used for static, non-time-sensitive content, such as the About Us page, Contact page, Privacy Policy, and other core informational pages.

Hierarchical Structure: Pages are organized hierarchically, allowing you to create parent and child pages to build a structured website with menus and submenus.

No Categories or Tags: Pages do not have categories or tags like posts. They are usually organized via menus.

Comments (Optional): By default, pages do not allow comments, but you can enable comments on individual pages if needed.

Not in RSS Feeds: Pages are not included in RSS feeds, as they are not typically part of regularly updated content.

2. Creating and Organizing Pages: To create and organize pages in WordPress:

Creating a New Page: In the WordPress dashboard, go to "Pages" > "Add New."

Enter a title for your page in the title field.

Add content to the main content area using the visual editor.

You can use formatting options, insert media, and add links just like in a word processor.

Click "Publish" to make the page live on your website.

Organizing Pages: You can create a hierarchical structure by setting parent and child pages. When editing a page, look for the "Page Attributes" box on the right-hand side.

To create a child page (a subpage), select a parent page from the "Parent" dropdown menu. This organizes your pages into a structured menu.

Creating a Menu: To display your pages in a specific order, create a menu in the WordPress dashboard by going to "Appearance" > "Menus."

Add your pages to the menu and arrange them as needed.

You can create multiple menus for different parts of your website, such as the main navigation menu, footer menu, or sidebar menu.

Custom Templates (Optional): Depending on your theme, you may have the option to choose different page templates for specific pages. For example, you might have a full-width template or a template with a sidebar.

Setting a Homepage: You can choose whether you want a specific page to be your website's homepage or display your latest posts. This can be configured in "Settings" > "Reading."

Pages are essential for providing static information about your site, while posts are used for dynamic, regularly updated content. By organizing pages effectively and creating a clear menu structure, you can ensure that visitors can easily navigate and access the information they need on your WordPress website.

Chapter 8: Customizing Your Website

Using the WordPress Customizer is a powerful way to make real-time changes to your website's appearance and settings. Here's how to use it to change your site title and tagline and set your homepage:

1. Accessing the WordPress Customizer To access the WordPress Customizer:

Log in to your WordPress dashboard.

In the admin toolbar on the front end of your website (when you're logged in), you'll see a "Customize" option. Click on it, and it will open the Customizer panel on the left side of your screen.

Alternatively, you can also access the Customizer from the WordPress dashboard. Go to "Appearance" > "Customize."

2. Changing Site Title and Tagline: Once you're in the WordPress Customizer, follow these steps to change your site title and tagline:

In the Customizer panel, you'll see various sections with options for customizing your site's appearance and settings.

To change your site title and tagline, look for a section typically labelled "Site Identity." Click on it to expand the options.

In the Site Identity section, you should see fields for "Site Title" and "Tagline." Click on these fields to edit them.

Enter your desired site title and tagline. These can be the name of your website or business and a brief description.

As you make changes, you should see them reflected in real-time on a preview of your website in the right-hand pane.

Once you've updated your site title and tagline, click the "Publish" button to save your changes.

3. Setting Your Homepage: To set your homepage in the WordPress Customizer:

In the Customizer panel, navigate to the "Homepage Settings" or "Static Front Page" section. This location may vary slightly depending on your theme.

In this section, you'll typically find options for setting your homepage. You can choose between two options:

Your Latest Posts: This option will display your most recent blog posts on the homepage.

A Static Page: This option allows you to select a specific page as your homepage and another page to display your blog posts (if you have a blog).

To set a static page as your homepage, select the "A Static Page" option and then choose the page you want to use as your homepage from the dropdown menu under "Homepage."

If you want to create a new page to serve as your homepage, you can do so by clicking the "+ New Page" link in the dropdown menu.

After selecting your homepage, you can also choose a page to display your blog posts if you have one. This is optional, and you can leave it as "Select" if you want your homepage to show your latest posts.

Once you've configured your homepage settings, click the "Publish" button to save your changes.

The WordPress Customizer provides a user-friendly way to make these essential changes to your site without needing to delve into the backend settings. It allows you to preview the changes before making them live, ensuring that your website looks and functions exactly as you want it to.

Chapter 9: Installing and Managing Plugins

W hat Are Plugins?

Plugins are pieces of software that you can add to your WordPress website to extend its functionality and add new features. They are like add-ons or modules that allow you to customize and enhance your website without the need for custom coding. WordPress plugins can be used to perform a wide range of tasks, from adding contact forms and social media sharing buttons to optimizing your site for search engines and creating e-commerce stores. Plugins are a fundamental part of what makes WordPress so flexible and versatile.

2. Finding and Installing Plugins: Here's how to find and install plugins on your WordPress website:

Finding Plugins: In your WordPress dashboard, go to "Plugins" > "Add New."

You'll see a search bar where you can enter keywords related to the type of plugin you're looking for. For example, if you want to add a contact form, you can search for "contact form."

Browse the search results to find plugins that match your needs. You can also filter by categories or browse popular and featured plugins.

Installing Plugins: Once you find a plugin you want to install, click the "Install Now" button next to it.

WordPress will download and install the plugin for you.

After installation, the "Install Now" button will change to an "Activate" button. Click "Activate" to enable the plugin on your site.

Configuring Plugins: Depending on the plugin, you may need to configure its settings. This can usually be done by going to "Plugins" > "Installed Plugins" and clicking on the plugin's name or settings link.

Follow the plugin's documentation or on-screen instructions to set it up according to your preferences.

3. Popular and Useful Plugins: WordPress has a vast ecosystem of plugins, so the ones you choose will depend on your specific needs. However, here are some popular and versatile plugins that many WordPress users find useful:

Yoast SEO: Helps with on-page SEO optimization, including meta tags, XML sitemaps, and content analysis.

WooCommerce: Transforms your WordPress website into a fully functional e-commerce store, allowing you to sell products and services online.

Contact Form 7: A simple and customizable plugin for creating contact forms and collecting user inquiries.

Akismet Anti-Spam: Protects your website from spam comments and submissions.

Jetpack: Offers a suite of features, including site statistics, social media sharing, contact forms, and more.

Wordfence Security: Enhances the security of your website by protecting against threats like malware and hacking attempts.

UpdraftPlus: Provides automated backups for your website, ensuring you can easily restore it if anything goes wrong.

WP Super Cache or W3 Total Cache: Caches your website to improve loading speed and performance.

Sucuri Security: A comprehensive security plugin for monitoring and protecting your site from various threats.

MonsterInsights: Integrates Google Analytics with your WordPress site, providing detailed insights into your website's performance.

Elementor or Beaver Builder: Page builder plugins that allow for easy drag-and-drop website design and customization.

Redirection: Helps manage 301 redirects, ensuring a seamless user experience and preserving SEO rankings when you change your site's structure or URLs.

These are just a few examples, and there are thousands of other plugins available to address specific needs and functionalities. When choosing plugins, it's essential to consider factors like user reviews, compatibility with your WordPress version, and regular updates to ensure they are secure and well-maintained.

Chapter 10: Understanding and Using Widgets

W hat Are Widgets?

In WordPress, widgets are small, pre-designed blocks or components that you can easily add to various areas of your website, typically the sidebar, footer, or other widget-ready areas. Widgets serve different purposes and provide specific functionalities without requiring you to write code. They allow you to customize the layout and content of your website, making it more engaging and user-friendly.

2. Adding Widgets to Your Sidebar or Footer:

To add widgets to your WordPress sidebar or footer, follow these general steps:

Access the Widget Customization Area: Log in to your WordPress dashboard.

Go to "Appearance" > "Widgets."

Choose a Widget Area: On the Widgets page, you'll see a list of available widget areas on your theme. Common areas include the sidebar, footer, and sometimes header.

Click on the widget area where you want to add widgets. For example, if you want to add widgets to the sidebar, click on "Sidebar."

Add Widgets: On the left-hand side, you'll find a list of available widgets. These may include standard WordPress widgets (e.g., Recent Posts, Categories) and widgets added by plugins you've installed.

To add a widget, drag it from the list on the left and drop it into the widget area on the right where you want it to appear.

Configure Widget Settings: After adding a widget, you can usually configure its settings by clicking on it within the widget area.

Settings will vary depending on the specific widget, but they typically include options like title, content, and display preferences.

Customize the settings to fit your needs.

Save Changes:

Click the "Save" or "Save Changes" button to apply your widget configurations.

Rearrange Widgets: To change the order of widgets in a widget area, simply drag and drop them into your desired order.

Remove Widgets: To remove a widget from a widget area, drag it back to the available widgets list, or click on it within the widget area and select "Delete" or "Remove."

Add More Widgets: You can add multiple widgets to a single widget area, and you can also use different widgets in different areas of your site.

3. Popular Widgets: The widgets available to you may vary based on your theme and any plugins you have installed. However, here are some commonly used and popular widgets in WordPress:

Recent Posts: Displays a list of your most recent blog posts.

Categories: Lists your website's categories, allowing users to navigate your content by topic.

Archives: Displays an archive list by month, helping users find older posts.

Search: Adds a search bar to your sidebar or footer, allowing visitors to search for specific content.

Text: Allows you to add custom text, HTML, or code to your widget area. This widget is highly versatile and can be used for various purposes.

Tag Cloud: Displays a list of tags used on your site, usually in a visually appealing cloud format.

Calendar: Shows a calendar highlighting dates with published posts.

Recent Comments: Lists the most recent comments on your site, encouraging engagement.

Social Media Icons: Allows you to add links to your social media profiles for easy access by visitors.

Popular Posts: Displays a list of your most popular posts based on views or other criteria.

Newsletter Signup: If you use an email marketing service, you can add a widget for visitors to subscribe to your newsletter.

These widgets can enhance the functionality and usability of your website, improving the overall user experience. Depending on your site's goals, you may want to use different combinations of widgets to achieve specific outcomes.

Chapter 11: Managing Comments

Enabling and disabling comments, moderating comments, and configuring comment settings are essential aspects of managing discussions and engagement on your WordPress website. Here's how to handle these tasks:

1. Enabling and Disabling Comments:

You can enable or disable comments globally for your entire WordPress site or on a per-post/page basis.

Global Setting (For the Entire Site):

Log in to your WordPress dashboard.

Go to "Settings" > "Discussion."

Under the "Default article settings" section, you'll see the option to "Allow people to post comments on new articles." Check or uncheck this option as needed.

Click the "Save Changes" button to update the global comment settings.

Per-Post/Per-Page Setting: While creating or editing a post or page, scroll down to the "Discussion" box in the editor's right-hand column.

You'll see a checkbox option to "Allow comments" for that specific post or page. Check or uncheck this option based on your preference.

Update or publish the post or page to save your comment settings.

2. Moderating Comments: Moderating comments allows you to review and approve or disapprove them before they appear on your website. Here's how to moderate comments:

Log in to your WordPress dashboard.

Go to "Comments" in the left-hand menu. You'll see a list of all comments on your site, including pending, approved, and spam comments.

Review the comments. You can hover over a comment to reveal options like "Approve," "Reply," "Edit," "Trash," and "Spam."

To approve a pending comment, click "Approve." Approved comments will be visible on your site.

To mark a comment as spam, click "Spam." This helps filter out unwanted or irrelevant comments.

To send a comment to the trash, click "Trash."

To reply to a comment, click "Reply" and enter your response.

You can also edit a comment by clicking "Edit" if needed.

After taking the appropriate action, be sure to click the "Save Changes" button to update the comment status.

3. Comment Settings: You can further customize comment settings to suit your preferences. Here are some key settings:

Comment Moderation: Under "Settings" > "Discussion," you can set criteria for moderating comments. For example, you can require that comments with multiple links or specific keywords be held for moderation.

Comment Blacklist: In the same "Discussion" settings, you can create a blacklist of words or IP addresses. Comments containing these words or from these addresses will be marked as spam automatically.

Avatar Display: You can enable or disable avatars for commenters. Avatars are often associated with Gravatar accounts.

Comment Notification: Decide whether you, as the site administrator, want to be notified via email when a new comment is posted.

Nested Comments: Determine if you want to enable threaded (nested) comments. This allows for more structured discussions.

Comment Count: Choose whether to display the comment count on your posts and pages.

By configuring these comment settings, you can create a commenting system that aligns with your website's goals, audience, and moderation preferences. Effective comment management can enhance user engagement while maintaining a respectful and spam-free   environment.

Chapter 12: Creating Navigation Menus

What Are Navigation Menus?

Navigation menus in WordPress are a crucial element of your website's structure. They are a collection of links that help visitors navigate your site, allowing them to access different sections or pages easily. Navigation menus are typically displayed in the header, footer, sidebar, or other designated areas of your WordPress theme.

2. Creating and Managing Menus: Here's how to create and manage navigation menus in WordPress:

Create a New Menu: Log in to your WordPress dashboard.

Go to "Appearance" > "Menus."

On the Menus page, you'll see a section where you can create a new menu. Enter a name for your menu (e.g., "Main Menu") and click the "Create Menu" button.

Add Items to Your Menu: After creating a menu, you can start adding items to it. On the left-hand side of the Menus page, you'll find a list of content types you can add to your menu, including Pages, Posts, Custom Links, and Categories.

To add items, select the content type you want to add, check the specific items (e.g., pages or categories) you want to include, and click the "Add to Menu" button.

Organize Menu Items: You can rearrange the order of menu items by dragging and dropping them into your preferred sequence.

To create submenus (dropdown menus), drag a menu item slightly to the right beneath another menu item. This action makes it a submenu item, appearing as a dropdown when you hover over the parent item on your site.

Customize Menu Items: Click on a menu item to expand its settings. Here, you can customize the label (the text displayed in the menu), the navigation label (what the user sees), and link target (whether it opens in the same or a new tab).

Remove Menu Items: To remove a menu item, click the arrow to expand its settings, and you'll find a "Remove" link. Click it to remove the item from your menu.

Manage Multiple Menus: If your theme supports multiple menus (e.g., a primary menu and a footer menu), you can create and manage them simultaneously on the Menus page.

Location Assignment: To display your menu on your website, you need to assign it to a specific location provided by your theme (e.g., "Primary Menu," "Footer Menu"). Locate the "Menu Settings" section on the Menus page and select the desired location for your menu.

Save Menu: After configuring your menu and assigning it to a location, don't forget to click the "Save Menu" button to save your changes.

3. Adding Pages, Categories, and Custom Links to Menus:

Adding Pages: To add pages to your menu, click the "Pages" tab on the left, select the pages you want to add, and click "Add to Menu."

Adding Categories: To add categories to your menu, click the "Categories" tab on the left, select the categories you want to add, and click "Add to Menu."

Adding Custom Links: To add custom links, click the "Custom Links" tab on the left. Here, you can enter the URL and link text for the custom link you want to add.

By creating and managing menus, you can ensure that your website's navigation is user-friendly and structured according to your content and site structure. Effective menus help visitors find the information they need quickly and improve their overall experience on your WordPress site.

Chapter 13: WordPress Settings

Configuring general settings, reading settings, and permalinks settings are important steps in setting up your WordPress website. These settings control various aspects of your site's appearance, behaviour, and URL structure. Here's how to configure each of these settings:

1. General Settings: General settings encompass basic information about your website, such as its title, tagline, and time zone. To configure general settings:

Log in to your WordPress dashboard.

Go to "Settings" > "General."

You will see several fields to configure:

Site Title: This is the name of your website, which will appear in the header or browser tab. It's usually your brand or website name.

Tagline (Optional): A brief description or slogan for your site. This can help convey your site's purpose.

WordPress Address (URL): This should be the directory where your WordPress core files are installed. In most cases, it's your site's domain (e.g., http://yourwebsite.com).

Site Address (URL): This is the URL where your site is accessible. It should also be your domain (e.g., http://yourwebsite.com).

Email Address: The admin email address for your site, where you'll receive notifications and password reset emails.

Membership (Optional): You can choose whether to allow people to register on your site. This setting is often used for membership or community websites.

New User Default Role: If you allow user registration, this setting determines the default role assigned to new users. "Subscriber" is the default, which allows them to comment.

Time zone: Select your site's time zone. This is important for scheduling posts and other time-related settings.

Date Format and Time Format: Customize how dates and times are displayed on your site.

After configuring these settings, click the "Save Changes" button at the bottom of the page to save your changes.

2. Reading Settings:

Reading settings control how your site's front page (homepage) and blog posts are displayed. To configure reading settings:

In your WordPress dashboard, go to "Settings" > "Reading."

You will see several options:

Your Homepage Displays: Choose between "Your latest posts" or "A static page."

If you choose "Your latest posts," your homepage will display your most recent blog posts.

If you choose "A static page," you can select a specific page as your homepage and another page for your blog posts.

Blog Pages Show at Most: Set the number of blog posts to display on your blog page.

Syndication Feeds Show the Most Recent: Set the number of blog posts to include in your RSS feed. This can be useful for subscribers who follow your content through RSS readers.

After configuring these settings, click the "Save Changes" button to save your changes.

3. Permalinks Settings: Permalinks determine the structure of URLs for your posts and pages. Customizing permalinks can improve SEO and make your URLs more user-friendly. To configure permalinks settings:

In your WordPress dashboard, go to "Settings" > "Permalinks."

You will see various common permalink structures to choose from. Some examples include:

Plain: This uses the default URL structure with post IDs.

Day and Name: Includes the date and post name in the URL.

Month and Name: Similar to "Day and Name," but without the day.

Post Name: This is a clean and SEO-friendly structure that includes only the post/page name in the URL.

Select the permalink structure that best suits your SEO and user experience goals.

After selecting a structure, click the "Save Changes" button to save your permalink settings.

Configuring these settings correctly ensures that your website has a professional appearance, proper functionality, and user-friendly URLs. It's an essential step in the initial setup of your WordPress site.

Chapter 14: User Management

Adding and managing users, along with understanding user roles and permissions, are essential aspects of running a WordPress website. Here's a guide on how to perform these tasks:

1. Adding and Managing Users: To add and manage users on your WordPress website:

Log in to your WordPress dashboard as an administrator.

Go to "Users" in the left-hand menu.

On the Users page, you'll see a list of existing users if you have any. To add a new user, click the "Add New" button.

Fill in the required user information, including:

Username: The username the user will use to log in.

Email: The user's email address. This will be used for notifications and password resets.

First Name and Last Name (optional): You can enter the user's real name.

Website (optional): The user's website URL.

Password: Set a secure password for the user or generate one automatically using the "Generate Password" button.

In the "Role" dropdown menu, select the appropriate user role for the new user (more on this below).

You can also choose to send a notification to the user with their login details by checking the "Send User Notification" box.

Finally, click the "Add New User" button to create the new user.

2. User Roles and Permissions:

WordPress has several predefined user roles, each with different permissions. Here's an overview of the common user roles:

Administrator: Administrators have full control over the website. They can add, delete, and modify content, themes, plugins, and users. They can also change website settings.

Editor: Editors can publish, edit, and delete their own and other users' posts and pages. They have control over content but cannot modify themes or plugins.

Author: Authors can publish, edit, and delete their own posts. They have control over their content but not others'.

Contributor: Contributors can write and edit their own posts but cannot publish them. They need approval from an editor or administrator to publish.

Subscriber: Subscribers can log in, edit their profile, and leave comments on your website. They have the least permissions.

You can assign roles when adding or editing a user. To change a user's role:

Go to "Users" in the WordPress dashboard.

Locate the user whose role you want to change and click "Edit" under their username.

In the "Role" dropdown menu, select the new role for the user.

Click the "Update User" button to save the changes.

It's essential to assign roles based on the user's responsibilities to maintain security and control over your website. Administrators should be trusted individuals, as they have the most power to modify your site.

Managing users and their roles allows you to collaborate effectively on your WordPress site, assign responsibilities, and control who can access and edit specific parts of your website.

Chapter 15: Media Library

Uploading and managing media, including images, is a fundamental part of running a WordPress website. Here's how to upload and manage media, set image sizes, and optimize your images for better performance:

1. Uploading and Managing Media: To upload and manage media in WordPress:

Log in to your WordPress dashboard.

Go to "Media" in the left-hand menu.

On the Media Library page, you'll see a list of all the media files (images, videos, audio) you've uploaded to your site. You can filter and search for media using the available options.

To upload new media, click the "Add New" button at the top of the page. You can either drag and drop files into the upload area or click the "Select Files" button to choose files from your computer.

After the upload is complete, you can add titles, descriptions, and alt text to the media files by clicking on them in the Media Library.

To insert media into posts or pages, you can click on the media file in the library, copy the URL, and paste it into your content editor. Alternatively, you can use the "Add Media" button when editing a post or page to insert media directly.

2. Image Sizes and Optimization: Properly managing image sizes and optimizing them is crucial for website performance and user experience. Here's how to handle this:

Image Sizes: WordPress generates multiple sizes of each image you upload (thumbnail, medium, large, and original). You can configure the default image sizes in the "Settings" > "Media" section of your WordPress dashboard. Adjust the maximum dimensions to suit your website's design and layout.

Some themes and plugins may add custom image sizes. To regenerate thumbnails for your images after changing image sizes, you can use plugins like "Regenerate Thumbnails."

When inserting images into your posts or pages, you can select the image size you want to use. WordPress will automatically create and serve the appropriate size based on your selection.

Image Optimization: Optimizing images helps reduce their file size while maintaining good quality, which improves website loading speed. You can optimize images before uploading using tools like Adobe Photoshop, GIMP, or online image compressors.

There are also WordPress plugins like "Smush" and "EWWW Image Optimizer" that can automatically compress and optimize images in your media library.

Use the "Alt Text" field when adding images to improve accessibility and SEO. Describe the image in a concise and relevant manner.

Consider using the WebP image format, which provides good quality at smaller file sizes. Some optimization plugins can automatically convert your images to WebP format.

Lazy Loading: Lazy loading is a technique that delays the loading of images until they are visible in the user's browser viewport. This can significantly improve page load times.

Many modern WordPress themes and optimization plugins support lazy loading. You can enable it in your theme settings or using a lazy loading plugin.

Optimizing your media files, managing image sizes, and implementing lazy loading are important steps for improving your website's performance, reducing server load, and providing a better experience for your users.

Chapter 16: WordPress Security

Securing your WordPress website is crucial to protect it from various threats and vulnerabilities. Here are essential security tips, including using security plugins and regular backups:

1. Essential Security Tips: Keep WordPress, Themes, and Plugins Updated: Regularly update your WordPress core, themes, and plugins to the latest versions. Developers often release updates to fix security vulnerabilities.

Use Strong Passwords: Enforce strong, unique passwords for all user accounts, especially the administrator account. Consider using a password manager to generate and store complex passwords.

Limit Login Attempts: Use a plugin to limit the number of login attempts. This helps prevent brute force attacks.

Enable Two-Factor Authentication (2FA): Implement 2FA for added security. This requires users to provide a second authentication method, such as a one-time code from a mobile app, in addition to their password.

Regularly Audit User Accounts: Review and remove any inactive or unnecessary user accounts, especially those with administrator privileges.

Change Default Admin Username: If your admin username is still "admin," change it to something unique. This reduces the risk of brute force attacks.

Install an SSL Certificate: Use HTTPS to encrypt data transmitted between your website and users' browsers. Many hosting providers offer free SSL certificates.

Limit File Permissions: Ensure that file and directory permissions are set correctly. Files should generally be set to 644, and directories to 755.

Install a Web Application Firewall (WAF): A WAF can help block malicious traffic and protect your website from various online threats.

Regularly Scan for Malware: Use a security plugin or online scanning tools to check for malware and vulnerabilities.

Disable Directory Listing: Disable directory listing to prevent hackers from seeing the contents of your directories.

Protect Your wp-config.php File: Add the following code to your .htaccess file to restrict access to your wp-config.php file:

```
<Files wp-config.php>
order allow,deny
deny from all
</Files>
```

2. Using Security Plugins: WordPress security plugins can enhance your site's security by offering features like firewall protection, malware scanning, login attempt limiting, and more. Some popular security plugins include:

Wordfence Security: Offers firewall protection, malware scanning, login security, and more.

Sucuri Security: Provides website firewall, malware scanning, and security hardening features.

iThemes Security (formerly Better WP Security): Offers a range of security enhancements, including brute force protection and file change detection.

All in One WP Security & Firewall: Provides an easy-to-use interface for enhancing security with various features.

Choose a security plugin that suits your needs and regularly update it to keep your site protected.

3. Regular Backups: Regular backups are essential for disaster recovery and security. They allow you to restore your website in case of data loss or security breaches. Here's how to set up regular backups:

Use a reputable backup plugin such as UpdraftPlus, BackWPup, or VaultPress (by Jetpack).

Configure the plugin to create automatic backups of your website at regular intervals (e.g., daily, weekly).

Store backups in a secure location, such as cloud storage or an external server.

Test your backups by restoring your website on a staging server to ensure they are working correctly.

By following these security tips, using security plugins, and maintaining regular backups, you can significantly enhance the security of your WordPress website and minimize the risk of security breaches and data loss.

Chapter 17: Search Engine Optimization (SEO)

SEO Basics: Search Engine Optimization (SEO) is a set of techniques and strategies used to improve your website's visibility in search engine results. Here are some fundamental SEO concepts:

Keywords: Identify relevant keywords and phrases related to your content. Use tools like Google Keyword Planner to find keywords with high search volume and relevance to your topic.

On-Page SEO: Optimize individual pages and posts by including keywords in the title, headings, meta descriptions, and content. Use descriptive alt text for images.

Quality Content: Create high-quality, engaging, and informative content that addresses the needs and interests of your target audience.

User Experience (UX): Ensure your website is user-friendly, loads quickly, and works well on mobile devices. Google considers user experience in its ranking algorithms.

Backlinks: Acquire high-quality backlinks (links from other websites to yours) to build authority and trust with search engines.

Technical SEO: Address technical issues like website speed, mobile-friendliness, and proper HTML markup.

2. Installing and Configuring an SEO Plugin (e.g., Yoast SEO): The Yoast SEO plugin is one of the most popular SEO plugins for WordPress. Here's how to install and configure it:

Log in to your WordPress dashboard.

Go to "Plugins" > "Add New."

Search for "Yoast SEO."

Click "Install Now" and then "Activate" to activate the plugin.

Once activated, you'll see a new "SEO" menu item in your dashboard. Click on it to access the plugin settings.

Follow the setup wizard provided by Yoast SEO to configure the plugin for your website. This includes setting your website's environment, choosing whether it's for a company or a personal blog, and verifying your site with search engines like Google.

After completing the setup wizard, you can access various features like meta title and description optimization, XML sitemap generation, and readability analysis for your content.

Customize the plugin settings to match your SEO goals and preferences. You can configure settings for titles and meta descriptions, social media sharing, and more.

3. Optimizing Content for SEO: Optimizing your content for SEO is a crucial aspect of improving your website's search engine rankings. Here are some tips:

Keyword Research: Conduct keyword research to identify relevant keywords for your content. Use tools like Google Keyword Planner or SEMrush to find keywords with good search volume and low competition.

Title Tag: Use your primary keyword in the title tag of your page or post. Make the title descriptive and engaging.

Meta Description: Write a compelling meta description that includes your primary keyword. This description should provide a concise summary of your content.

Headings (H1, H2, H3, etc.): Use headings to structure your content. Include your primary keyword in at least one heading (usually the H1) and use subheadings (H2, H3, etc.) to break up content into sections.

Content Quality: Create high-quality, informative, and engaging content. Focus on providing value to your readers.

Internal Linking: Link to other relevant pages or posts on your website where it makes sense. This helps improve site navigation and SEO.

Image Optimization: Use descriptive alt text for images, and compress images to reduce page load times.

URL Structure: Create clean and descriptive URLs for your pages and posts. Include keywords when possible.

Mobile Optimization: Ensure your website is mobile-friendly, as mobile usability is a significant ranking factor.

Readability: Use short paragraphs, bullet points, and simple language to make your content easy to read.

Publish Consistently: Regularly update your website with fresh, valuable content. Search engines favour websites that are active and current.

External Links: When appropriate, link to authoritative and relevant external sources. This can improve the credibility of your content.

Remember that SEO is an ongoing process, and it may take time to see significant results. Regularly monitor your website's performance using tools like Google Analytics and Search Console, and make adjustments to your SEO strategy as needed.

Chapter 18: Performance Optimization

Improving website speed is crucial for providing a better user experience and positively impacting search engine rankings. Here are key strategies for optimizing your website's speed, including caching and minification, and utilizing Content Delivery Networks (CDNs):

1. Improving Website Speed: Optimize Images: Large images can slow down your site. Use image compression tools and ensure images are the right size for their display.

Enable Browser Caching: Browser caching allows browsers to store static resources like images, CSS, and JavaScript files locally, reducing load times for returning visitors.

Minimize HTTP Requests: Reduce the number of requests your website makes to the server by combining and minifying CSS and JavaScript files.

Use a Content Delivery Network (CDN): CDNs distribute your website's content across multiple servers worldwide, reducing latency and speeding up content delivery.

Reduce Server Response Time: Choose a reliable hosting provider, use caching plugins, and optimize your website's code to reduce server response times.

Use a Fast Theme/Template: Choose a lightweight and well-coded theme or template for your website.

Limit External Scripts: Minimize the use of external scripts and third-party widgets that can slow down your site.

Enable GZIP Compression: GZIP compression reduces file sizes before sending them to the browser, saving bandwidth and improving load times.

Lazy Load Content: Implement lazy loading for images and videos so they load only when they come into the user's viewport.

2. Caching and Minification: Caching: Caching is the process of storing frequently accessed data or files in a cache. In WordPress,

caching plugins like W3 Total Cache, WP Super Cache, or WP Rocket can be used to create and manage caches. These plugins generate static HTML files that can be served to users, reducing the need to repeatedly generate pages dynamically.

Minification: Minification involves removing unnecessary characters (such as white spaces, line breaks, and comments) from your HTML, CSS, and JavaScript files to reduce their file sizes. This makes your site load faster. Popular plugins like Auto optimize can help with minification.

3. Content Delivery Networks (CDNs): A Content Delivery Network (CDN) is a network of servers distributed around the world that store cached copies of your website's static assets (e.g., images, CSS, JavaScript). Here's how to use a CDN:

Select a CDN Provider: Choose a CDN provider like Cloudflare, Amazon CloudFront, or Max CDN.

Sign Up and Configure: Sign up for the CDN service and follow their setup instructions. You'll typically need to configure your DNS settings to route traffic through the CDN.

Install a CDN Plugin (Optional): Some CDN providers offer WordPress plugins for easy integration. These plugins automate the process of connecting your site to the CDN.

Cache Static Assets: Configure the CDN to cache and serve your website's static assets. The CDN will distribute these assets to its server locations worldwide.

SSL Configuration: If your site uses SSL, ensure that your CDN supports it, and configure it correctly to avoid mixed content issues.

Monitor Performance: Regularly monitor your website's performance with the CDN in place. CDNs often provide analytics and performance metrics.

A well-configured CDN can significantly reduce the load times of your website for visitors from various geographical locations, making it an excellent investment for improving user experience and SEO.

Chapter 19: Troubleshooting and Common Issues

Common WordPress problems, debugging and error handling, and finding help and support are essential aspects of managing a WordPress website. Here's a guide to address these areas:

1. Common WordPress Problems:

a. White Screen of Death (WSOD): This is when your site displays a blank white page. It can be caused by PHP errors, memory issues, or conflicts with plugins or themes.

Solution: Disable recently installed plugins or themes, increase PHP memory limits, or check error logs for specific issues.

b. Plugin or Theme Compatibility Issues: Some plugins or themes may not work well together or with specific versions of WordPress.

Solution: Deactivate plugins or themes one by one to identify the problematic one. Update or replace outdated plugins or themes.

c. WordPress Updates Breaking the Site: Occasionally, updating WordPress or plugins can lead to compatibility issues.

Solution: Create backups before updating, and test updates in a staging environment first. Roll back updates if issues arise.

d. Security Breaches: Hacks, malware, and security vulnerabilities can compromise your site's integrity.

Solution: Regularly update WordPress, themes, and plugins. Use security plugins, strong passwords, and consider a website firewall. Scan for malware regularly.

e. Slow Loading Times: Slow loading can be due to large images, too many plugins, or server issues.

Solution: Optimize images, reduce unnecessary plugins, and consider upgrading your hosting plan for better server performance.

2. Debugging and Error Handling:

a. Enable WordPress Debug Mode: You can enable debug mode to see PHP errors on your site. Edit your site's wp-config.php file and set WP_DEBUG to true:

```
define('WP_DEBUG', true);
```

Additionally, you can define where the debug log is saved with:

```
define('WP_DEBUG_LOG', true);
define('WP_DEBUG_DISPLAY', false);
```

This way, errors are logged but not displayed to visitors.

b. Error Messages: When you encounter an error, WordPress often provides specific error messages. Use these messages to pinpoint the issue.

c. Check Server Error Logs: If you have access to your server's error logs (usually available in your hosting control panel), review them for error messages that can help identify issues.

3. Finding Help and Support:

a. WordPress.org Forums: The WordPress.org support forums are a valuable resource. You can ask questions, search for answers to common issues, and interact with the community.

b. Official Documentation: The WordPress Codex and Handbook provide extensive documentation on various aspects of WordPress, including troubleshooting and development.

c. Plugin and Theme Support: If you're experiencing issues with a specific plugin or theme, reach out to its developer or support team for assistance. Most premium themes and plugins offer support forums or ticket systems.

d. social media and WordPress Communities: Platforms like Twitter, Facebook, and LinkedIn have WordPress-related groups and communities where you can seek advice and assistance.

e. Hire a WordPress Developer: If you're unable to resolve a complex issue or need customization, consider hiring a WordPress developer or a WordPress support service.

f. WordPress Meetups and Word Camps: Attend local WordPress meetups or virtual Word Camps to connect with experts and enthusiasts who can offer advice and solutions.

g. Professional WordPress Support Services: Some companies and individuals offer professional WordPress support services for troubleshooting, maintenance, and optimization.

When facing WordPress problems, it's essential to approach them systematically, back up your site before making changes, and seek help when needed. The WordPress community and resources are vast, so don't hesitate to reach out for assistance.

Chapter 20: Website Launch and Beyond

After setting up your WordPress website, there are several important steps to ensure it's ready for public viewing, maintain its performance, and keep it up to date. Here's a guide to final testing, announcing your website, and ongoing maintenance and updates:

1. Final Testing:

Before announcing your website to the public, thorough testing is crucial to identify and resolve any issues. Here's what to check during final testing:

Cross-Browser Compatibility: Test your website in various web browsers (e.g., Chrome, Firefox, Safari, Edge) to ensure it looks and functions correctly.

Responsiveness: Verify that your site is mobile-friendly and displays well on different devices, including smartphones and tablets.

Links and Navigation: Check that all links are working correctly, including internal and external links. Test your site's navigation to ensure it's intuitive and functional.

Forms: Test any contact forms, comment forms, or other interactive elements to make sure they work as expected.

Load Time: Check the website's load time to ensure it's fast. Tools like Google PageSpeed Insights or GTmetrix can help you identify performance bottlenecks.

Spelling and Grammar: Proofread your content to catch any spelling or grammar mistakes.

Functionality: Test any interactive features, such as search functionality, shopping carts, and member logins.

SEO: Ensure that your SEO settings are in place and that your website is correctly indexed by search engines.

Security: Review your website's security settings and consider running a security scan to identify vulnerabilities.

2. Announcing Your Website: Once you've thoroughly tested your website and are satisfied with its performance, it's time to make it public. Here's how to announce your website:

Remove Under Construction Notices: If you had an "under construction" or "coming soon" page, remove it to make your site accessible to visitors.

Submit Your Site to Search Engines: Use Google Search Console and Bing Webmaster Tools to submit your website for indexing by search engines.

Promote on social media: Share your website on your social media profiles and encourage your followers to visit.

Email Newsletter: If you have an email subscriber list, send out a newsletter announcing your new website.

Press Release: Consider sending a press release if your website launch is significant or relevant to a particular industry.

Engage With Your Audience: Be prepared to engage with visitors and respond to comments or inquiries promptly.

3. Ongoing Maintenance and Updates: To ensure the long-term success of your website, ongoing maintenance and updates are essential:

Content Updates: Regularly update and add new content to keep your website fresh and engaging.

Security: Keep WordPress, themes, and plugins up to date to patch security vulnerabilities. Use security plugins to monitor and protect your site.

Backups: Maintain regular backups of your website's data and files.

Performance Monitoring: Continuously monitor your site's performance and address any issues that may arise.

SEO: Regularly review and update your SEO strategy to improve search engine rankings.

User Feedback: Listen to user feedback and make improvements based on suggestions and comments.

Review Analytics: Analyse website analytics to understand user behaviour and make data-driven decisions.

Legal Compliance: Ensure that your website complies with legal requirements, such as GDPR for data protection or accessibility standards.

Regular Testing: Periodically perform website testing to catch and address any issues that may arise.

By following these steps, you can successfully launch your WordPress website, maintain its performance and security, and continue to improve its user experience over time. Remember that a well-maintained and up-to-date website is more likely to attract and retain visitors.

Chapter 21: Security Best Practices

Securing your WordPress website is critical to protect it from common security threats. Here's a guide on identifying common threats, implementing security measures in themes and plugins, and hardening your WordPress installation:

Identifying Common Security Threats: Brute Force Attacks: Attackers try to guess your admin login credentials by repeatedly attempting different username and password combinations.

SQL Injection: Hackers manipulate input fields to execute malicious SQL queries, potentially gaining unauthorized access to your database.

Cross-Site Scripting (XSS): Malicious scripts are injected into your site's content, which can be executed by visitors, compromising their data or stealing session information.

Cross-Site Request Forgery (CSRF): Attackers trick users into executing malicious actions on a site where they are authenticated, potentially leading to unauthorized actions being taken on their behalf.

File Inclusion Vulnerabilities: Hackers exploit vulnerabilities in plugins or themes to include malicious files that can harm your site.

Outdated Software: Using outdated WordPress core, plugins, or themes can expose your site to known vulnerabilities.

Implementing Security Measures in Themes and Plugins: Keep Themes and Plugins Updated: Regularly update your themes and plugins to the latest versions to patch security vulnerabilities. Remove any inactive or unnecessary themes and plugins.

Use Reputable Themes and Plugins: Only download themes and plugins from trusted sources like the WordPress.org repository or reputable commercial vendors. Avoid "nulled" themes and plugins.

Minimize Plugins: Use a minimal number of plugins to reduce the attack surface. Disable and delete any unused plugins.

Regular Code Audits: If you develop your themes or plugins, conduct regular code audits to identify and fix vulnerabilities.

Implement Input Validation and Sanitization: Ensure that all user inputs are validated and sanitized to prevent SQL injection and XSS attacks.

Strong Password Policies: Enforce strong password policies for user accounts. Limit login attempts to prevent brute force attacks.

Hardening Your WordPress Installation: Change Default Admin Username: Avoid using the default "admin" username. Create a unique username for the administrator account.

Use Strong Passwords: Use strong, complex passwords for all user accounts, especially administrator accounts. Consider implementing two-factor authentication (2FA).

Secure wp-config.php: Protect your wp-config.php file by placing it outside the webroot and setting appropriate permissions. Add security rules to your .htaccess file.

Limit Login Attempts: Use a plugin to limit the number of login attempts. This discourages brute force attacks.

Disable XML-RPC: XML-RPC can be a target for attacks. If not needed, consider disabling it with a security plugin.

Install a Security Plugin: Consider using a security plugin like Wordfence, Sucuri Security, or iThemes Security to monitor and protect your site.

Regular Backups: Perform regular backups of your website and store them securely. These can be a lifesaver in case of a security breach.

Content Security Policy (CSP): Implement a CSP header to prevent XSS attacks by specifying which domains can load resources on your site.

Monitor File Changes: Set up file integrity monitoring to receive alerts when files are modified or added.

Web Application Firewall (WAF): Consider using a WAF to filter out malicious traffic before it reaches your website.

By identifying common security threats, implementing security measures in your themes and plugins, and hardening your WordPress installation, you can significantly reduce the risk of security breaches and keep your website safe and secure. Regular monitoring and updates are key to maintaining a secure WordPress site.

Chapter 23: Multilingual and Internationalization

Making your WordPress site multilingual is essential if you want to reach a global audience. Here's a guide on how to achieve this by using plugins like WPML or Polylang, implementing internationalization for themes and plugins, and managing translations:

1. Making Your Site Multilingual with WPML or Polylang:

WPML (WordPress Multilingual) and Polylang are popular plugins for creating multilingual websites in WordPress.

Using WPML: Install and activate the WPML plugin from the WordPress Plugin Repository.

Go through the initial setup process, where you'll choose the default language and the additional languages you want to support.

Translate your content: WPML allows you to translate posts, pages, custom post types, taxonomies, and more. You can either manually translate content or use professional translation services integrated with WPML.

Create language switchers: WPML provides widgets and shortcodes to add language switchers to your site, allowing users to select their preferred language.

SEO compatibility: WPML ensures that your translated content is SEO-friendly, making it easier for users to find your site in their preferred language.

Using Polylang: Install and activate the Polylang plugin from the WordPress Plugin Repository.

Set your default language and add additional languages in the Polylang settings.

Translate your content: Polylang allows you to translate posts, pages, categories, tags, and more. You can create translation relationships between content items.

Add language switchers: Polylang provides widgets and shortcodes for language switchers. You can customize the appearance and location of these switchers.

SEO compatibility: Polylang works well with popular SEO plugins like Yoast SEO to ensure multilingual SEO optimization.

2. Implementing Internationalization (i18n) for Themes and Plugins:

To make your themes and plugins translation-ready for multilingual websites, follow these steps:

Prepare Text Strings: Replace all hardcoded text strings in your theme or plugin files with translatable functions. For example, replace echo 'Hello World'; with echo __('Hello World', 'your-text-domain');.

Use the Text Domain: Specify a unique text domain for your theme or plugin. It's a best practice to use the same text domain throughout your code files.

Load Translation Files: Use WordPress functions like load_plugin_textdomain or load_theme_textdomain to load translation files. These files contain translations for different languages.

Provide a POT File: Create a .pot file for your theme or plugin. This file contains all the translatable text strings and serves as a template for translators.

Include Translations: Include .po and .mo translation files for each supported language in your theme or plugin's folder structure.

Document for Translators: Make it easy for translators to work on your project by providing clear instructions on how to create and submit translations.

3. Managing Translations: Once your themes and plugins are internationalized and translations are available, you need to manage them effectively:

Use Translation Tools: Consider using translation management tools like Poedit or online translation platforms like GlotPress for collaborative translation efforts.

Keep Translations Updated: Whenever you release updates to your themes or plugins, make sure to include any new text strings in your .pot file and update existing translations.

Provide Support for Translators: Offer support to translators by answering questions and clarifying context if needed. Clear communication with your translation team can result in more accurate translations.

Regularly Test Translations: Ensure that translations fit well within your theme or plugin's user interface and that there are no layout or formatting issues.

By making your site multilingual, internationalizing your themes and plugins, and effectively managing translations, you can create a user-friendly experience for visitors from different language backgrounds, helping your website reach a broader audience.

Chapter 24: Building Custom Post Types and Taxonomies

Understanding post types and taxonomies is fundamental in WordPress development, especially when you want to create custom content structures. Here's a guide on these topics, including creating custom post types and extending content organization with custom taxonomies:

Understanding Post Types and Taxonomies:

Post Types: In WordPress, "post types" define the type of content on your site. The default post types include "Posts" (for blog posts) and "Pages" (for static content like the About Us page).

Custom post types allow you to create new content structures with their own templates and features. For example, you can create "Portfolio" or "Testimonials" post types.

Taxonomies: Taxonomies are ways to categorize and organize content. WordPress has two default taxonomies: categories and tags, which are used to classify posts.

Custom taxonomies allow you to create additional ways to classify content. For example, you could create a "Genre" taxonomy for a "Books" custom post type.

Creating Custom Post Types: To create a custom post type in WordPress, follow these steps:

Functions.php File: Open your theme's functions.php file (or create a custom plugin for this purpose).

Register the Custom Post Type: Use the register_post_type() function to define your custom post type. Here's an example for a "Portfolio" post type:

```
function create_portfolio_post_type() {
    register_post_type('portfolio',
        array(
            'labels' => array(
                'name' => __('Portfolio'),
                'singular_name' => __('Portfolio Item'),
            ),
            'public' => true,
            'has_archive' => true,
            'rewrite' => array('slug' => 'portfolio'),
            'supports' => array('title', 'editor', 'thumbnail', 'custom-fields'),
        )
    );
}
add_action('init', 'create_portfolio_post_type');
```

In the example above, we define the post type's labels, visibility, archive, rewrite rules, and supported features.

Flush Rewrite Rules: After adding or modifying custom post types, flush the rewrite rules by visiting Settings > Permalinks in your WordPress dashboard and simply clicking "Save Changes."

Content Entry: Now you can start adding content of your custom post type via the WordPress dashboard.

Extending Content Organization with Custom Taxonomies: To extend content organization with custom taxonomies, follow these steps:

Functions.php File: Open your theme's functions.php file (or create a custom plugin for this purpose).

Register the Custom Taxonomy: Use the register_taxonomy() function to define your custom taxonomy. Here's an example for a "Genre" taxonomy:

```
function create_genre_taxonomy() {
    register_taxonomy(
        'genre',
        'book',
        array(
            'label' => __('Genre'),
            'hierarchical' => true,
            'public' => true,
            'rewrite' => array('slug' => 'genre'),
        )
    );
}
add_action('init', 'create_genre_taxonomy');
```

In the example above, we define the taxonomy's label, hierarchy (whether it should be like categories or tags), visibility, and rewrite rules.

Attach Taxonomy to a Post Type: To associate the custom taxonomy with a custom post type, use the register_taxonomy_for_object_type() function. For example, to associate "Genre" with the "Books" post type:

```
function attach_genre_to_books() {
    register_taxonomy_for_object_type('genre', 'book');
}
add_action('init', 'attach_genre_to_books');
```

Content Entry: Now, when you edit or create a "Books" post, you can assign genres just like you would with categories or tags.

By creating custom post types and taxonomies, you can structure your content in a way that makes sense for your specific website, improving both user experience and content organization. This flexibility is one of WordPress's strengths as a CMS.

Chapter 25: User Authentication and Roles

Managing user accounts and profiles, implementing custom login and registration forms, and customizing user roles and permissions are crucial aspects of WordPress when building community-driven or membership-based websites. Here's a guide on how to handle these tasks effectively:

Managing User Accounts and Profiles:

User Registration Settings: In your WordPress dashboard, navigate to "Settings" > "General."

Ensure that the "Membership" or "Anyone can register" option is enabled, allowing users to register on your site.

User Roles: WordPress has predefined user roles, such as Administrator, Editor, Author, Contributor, and Subscriber.

Users can be assigned roles based on their responsibilities and access levels.

User Registration Plugins: You can enhance user registration and profile management by using plugins like "Profile Builder," "User Registration," or "Ultimate Member." These plugins allow you to create custom registration and profile update forms.

Implementing Custom Login and Registration Forms:

Custom Registration Form: Use a plugin like "User Registration" or "Profile Builder" to create custom registration forms.

Customize the form fields to collect the information you need, such as username, email, name, and additional profile details.

Custom Login Form: You can create a custom login form using plugins like "Custom Login Page Customizer" or by modifying your theme's template files.

Embed the login form on a dedicated login page or in a widget.

Short codes: Many registration and login plugins provide short codes that allow you to easily insert forms on any page or post.

Custom Styling: Customize the appearance of your forms to match your website's design using CSS.

Customizing User Roles and Permissions:

Roles and Capabilities: You can customize user roles and capabilities using plugins or custom code.

Plugins like "Members" and "User Role Editor" simplify role management.

Custom Roles: Create custom roles if the default roles don't fit your needs.

For custom roles, define the specific capabilities users in that role should have.

Custom Permissions: Fine-tune permissions by adding or removing capabilities from roles.

Use custom code in your theme's functions.php file or a custom plugin to modify permissions.

Access Control for Content: Use access control plugins like "Members" or "Restrict Content Pro" to restrict content based on user roles and capabilities.

Set permissions for pages, posts, or custom post types.

Role-Based Content: Create content that's visible only to specific user roles using conditional statements in your theme templates or content editor.

Role-Based Redirects: Redirect users after login based on their roles using plugins like "Peter's Login Redirect" or custom code.

User Profile Fields: Customize user profiles by adding custom fields for each user role.

Use plugins like "Advanced Custom Fields" or custom code to add and display these fields.

By effectively managing user accounts, customizing registration and login forms, and fine-tuning user roles and permissions, you can create a tailored user experience for your WordPress website, whether it's a community forum, membership site, or any other type of user-centric platform.

Chapter 26: E-commerce with WooCommerce

WooCommerce is a powerful e-commerce plugin for WordPress that enables you to set up and run an online store. Here's a guide that introduces WooCommerce, explains how to set up an online store, and extends WooCommerce with custom functionality:

1. Introduction to WooCommerce: What is WooCommerce? WooCommerce is a free, open-source WordPress plugin that adds e-commerce functionality to your website. It allows you to sell products or services online.

Key Features:

Product management: Create and manage products, including physical and digital goods.

Shopping cart: Provides a user-friendly shopping cart for customers to add and manage items.

Checkout process: Securely handles payments, shipping, and tax calculations.

Inventory management: Tracks stock levels and alerts for low inventory.

Payment gateways: Supports various payment methods, including PayPal, Stripe, and more.

Extensibility: Allows you to add extensions and custom functionality to meet specific needs.

2. Setting up an Online Store with WooCommerce:

Install WooCommerce: From your WordPress dashboard, navigate to "Plugins" > "Add New."

Search for "WooCommerce" and click "Install Now."

Activate the plugin.

WooCommerce Setup Wizard: Upon activation, WooCommerce guides you through a setup wizard.

Configure essential settings, including currency, payment methods, and shipping options.

Adding Products: Create product listings with details such as title, description, price, and images.

Categorize products and assign tags for easy navigation.

Setting Up Shipping: Configure shipping options, including flat-rate, free shipping, or real-time rates from carriers like UPS or FedEx.

Payment Methods: Enable payment gateways like PayPal, Stripe, credit cards, and more.

Configure payment settings and ensure secure transactions.

Tax Settings:

Set up tax rates and rules based on your location and products.

Additional Settings: Customize store settings, including email notifications, privacy policy, and terms and conditions.

Theme Compatibility: Ensure your WordPress theme is compatible with WooCommerce, or consider using a WooCommerce-specific theme for optimal e-commerce functionality.

3. Extending WooCommerce with Custom Functionality:

Use WooCommerce Extensions: WooCommerce offers a vast library of official and third-party extensions to add functionality. These can range from payment gateways to product add-ons and more.

Custom Development: For unique requirements, consider custom development.

Create custom product types, checkout fields, or reports tailored to your business needs.

Hooks and Filters: WooCommerce provides hooks and filters that allow developers to modify its behaviour.

You can add custom code to your theme's functions.php file or create a custom plugin to extend WooCommerce's functionality.

API Integration: Integrate WooCommerce with third-party services or platforms using its REST API. This is helpful for syncing data or creating custom workflows.

Performance Optimization: Optimize your WooCommerce store for speed and performance to provide a smooth shopping experience for customers.

User Experience Enhancements: Implement features like product reviews, wish lists, or product recommendations to improve the user experience.

Inventory and Order Management: Create custom solutions for advanced inventory management, order processing, or reporting if needed.

WooCommerce provides a robust foundation for building and running an online store. Whether you're selling physical products, digital downloads, or services, WooCommerce can be tailored to meet your specific e-commerce needs, making it a popular choice for businesses of all sizes.

Chapter 27: Theme Development Basics

Creating a basic WordPress theme is an essential skill for customizing the look and functionality of your WordPress website. Understanding the template hierarchy and enqueuing styles and scripts are fundamental aspects of theme development.

By following these steps, you can create a basic WordPress theme, understand the template hierarchy for displaying content, and enqueuing styles and scripts to control your theme's appearance and functionality. This provides a solid foundation for custom theme development in WordPress.

1. Creating a Basic WordPress Theme: To create a basic WordPress theme, follow these steps:

Step 1: Create a Theme Directory:

In your WordPress installation, navigate to the "wp-content/themes" directory.

Create a new folder for your theme. Give it a unique name, preferably one that describes your theme.

Step 2: Create the Theme Files: At a minimum, your theme should have two files: style.css and index.php.

style.css: This file contains the theme's metadata and styles. You can add a theme name, author information, and a description. Here's an example:

```
/*
Theme Name: Your Theme Name
Author: Your Name
Description: Description of your theme.
*/


/* Your CSS styles go here */
```

index.php: This is the main template file that WordPress will use to display your content. It should contain the basic structure of your theme, including HTML, PHP, and WordPress template tags.

Step 3: Activate Your Theme: Go to the WordPress dashboard.

Navigate to "Appearance" > "Themes."

Find your theme and click "Activate" to make it the active theme for your website.

Step 4: Customize Your Theme:

Edit the index.php file to customize your theme's layout, design, and functionality.

You can create additional template files for specific types of content (e.g., single.php for single posts, page.php for single pages) to control how different content is displayed.

2. Template Hierarchy and Template Files:

WordPress follows a template hierarchy to determine which template file to use for displaying different types of content. Understanding this hierarchy is crucial for theme development. Here are some common template files and their purposes:

index.php: The default template file used for displaying the homepage and other content when no specific template file is available.

single.php: Used for displaying single posts.

page.php: Used for displaying single pages.

archive.php: Used for displaying archive pages, such as category, tag, or date archives.

category.php: Used for displaying category archives.

tag.php: Used for displaying tag archives.

author.php: Used for displaying author archives.

search.php: Used for displaying search results.

404.php: Used for displaying the "Page Not Found" error.

To create custom template files for specific content types, follow the WordPress template hierarchy by naming the file according to the type you want to customize (e.g., single-{posttype}.php or category-{slug}.php).

3. Enqueuing Styles and Scripts:

To load your theme's styles and scripts properly, use the wp_enqueue_style and wp_enqueue_script functions in your theme's functions.php file. For example:

```
function enqueue_theme_styles() {
    wp_enqueue_style('your-theme-style', get_stylesheet_uri());
}
add_action('wp_enqueue_scripts', 'enqueue_theme_styles');

function enqueue_theme_scripts() {
    wp_enqueue_script('your-theme-script', get_template_directory_uri() . '/js/your-script.j
}
add_action('wp_enqueue_scripts', 'enqueue_theme_scripts');
```

wp_enqueue_style: This function loads your theme's stylesheets.

wp_enqueue_script: This function loads your theme's JavaScript files.

Ensure that you replace 'your-theme-style' and 'your-theme-script' with unique handles for your styles and scripts, and adjust the file paths accordingly.

Chapter 28: Plugin Development Essentials

Introduction to WordPress Plugins: WordPress plugins are pieces of software that add specific functionality or features to your WordPress website. They allow you to extend and enhance the capabilities of your site without modifying the core WordPress code. Plugins can be used to add contact forms, create e-commerce stores, optimize SEO, enhance security, and much more. They are an essential part of the WordPress ecosystem and provide a way to customize your site to meet your specific needs.

Hooks and Filters in WordPress: Hooks and filters are fundamental concepts in WordPress that enable you to modify and extend the functionality of your site. They allow you to "hook" into various points in the WordPress core code and apply custom code or "filter" data before it's displayed. Here's an overview:

Hooks: There are two types of hooks in WordPress: actions and filters.

Actions: Actions allow you to add custom functionality at specific points in the WordPress execution process. For example, you can use the wp_enqueue_scripts action to add styles and scripts to your site's header.

Filters: Filters enable you to modify data before it's displayed on your site. For instance, you can use the the_content filter to alter the content of posts or pages before they are rendered.

Customizing with Hooks and Filters: You can customize your WordPress site by creating custom functions and attaching them to hooks or filters.

These custom functions can be added to your theme's functions.php file or to a custom plugin.

Building a Simple Custom Plugin: Creating a custom plugin in WordPress is a powerful way to add specific functionality to your site. Here's how to build a simple custom plugin:

Create a Plugin Directory: In your WordPress installation, navigate to the "wp-content/plugins" directory.

Create a new folder for your plugin and give it a unique, descriptive name.

Create the Main Plugin File: Inside your plugin directory, create a PHP file (e.g., my-custom-plugin.php). This will be the main file for your plugin.

Define Plugin Information: In the main plugin file, start with the plugin header, which includes information about your plugin. Here's an example:

```php
<?php
/*
Plugin Name: My Custom Plugin
Description: This is a simple custom plugin for WordPress.
Version: 1.0
Author: Your Name
*/

// Plugin code goes here
```

Add Your Plugin Code: Write the functionality you want to add to your plugin. This can include hooks, filters, custom functions, or any PHP code specific to your needs.

Activate Your Plugin: In the WordPress dashboard, navigate to "Plugins."

Find your plugin in the list and click "Activate" to enable it.

Testing and Debugging: Test your plugin thoroughly to ensure it works as expected.

Use tools like error logs and WordPress debugging modes for troubleshooting if needed.

Publish and Share (Optional): If your plugin serves a broader audience, you can publish it in the official WordPress Plugin Repository, making it accessible to other WordPress users.

This is a basic outline of creating a custom plugin. Depending on your requirements, your plugin can become more complex with additional features and settings. Remember to follow best practices, sanitize user input, and document your plugin for yourself and potential   users.

Chapter 29: Building Custom Widgets

Introduction to Widgets: Widgets are small blocks of content or functionality that can be added to specific areas, usually sidebars, in your WordPress theme. They provide an easy way to customize and add dynamic elements to your website without the need for coding skills. Widgets can display anything from recent posts and categories to search bars and custom content.

Here are some key points about widgets: Widgets are usually used in widget-ready areas, commonly found in the sidebar, footer, and other widgetized sections of your theme.

WordPress comes with a set of built-in widgets, such as Recent Posts, Categories, and Archives.

You can also install plugins that add new widgets to your site, expanding the available options.

Creating Custom Widgets: Creating custom widgets allows you to add unique functionality or display specific content in widget areas. Here's an overview of how to create custom widgets:

Create a Custom Widget Class: Start by creating a PHP class that extends the WP_Widget class. This class will define your widget's behavior and appearance.

Define Widget Properties: In your custom widget class, define properties like the widget's name, description, and widget options (such as widget ID base).

Implement Widget Logic: Override the widget method to specify what your widget should display on the front end.

Implement Form Logic: Override the form and update methods to define how the widget's settings are configured and updated in the WordPress dashboard.

Register the Widget: Use the widgets_init action hook to register your custom widget class.

Instantiate the Widget: In the widget method, output the widget's content as needed. You can use HTML, PHP, or even call other functions to generate the content.

Adding Widgets to Your Theme: To add widgets to your theme's widget areas (usually sidebars), follow these steps:

Select a Widget Area: Decide where you want to display your widget. Common areas include the sidebar, footer, and any other widgetized sections in your theme.

Navigate to Widget Settings: In the WordPress dashboard, go to "Appearance" > "Widgets."

Drag and Drop Widgets: On the Widgets page, you'll see available widgets on the left and widget areas on the right. Drag and drop the widget you want to use into the chosen widget area.

Configure Widget Settings: Once you've added the widget, configure its settings, such as titles, content, and other options.

Save Changes: Click "Save" to apply your changes.

Now, your custom widget will appear in the selected widget area on the front end of your website.

Building Shortcodes: Shortcodes are another way to add dynamic content and functionality to your WordPress site. They are short pieces of text enclosed in square brackets (e.g., [shortcode]) and can be used in post content, pages, widgets, and even template files.

Here's how to create and use shortcodes in WordPress:

Understanding Shortcodes:

Shortcodes are placeholders for dynamic content generated by WordPress or custom functions.

WordPress comes with built-in shortcodes like [gallery] for displaying image galleries.

Shortcodes are processed when content is displayed on the front end, allowing for dynamic content insertion.

Creating Custom Shortcodes for Content Display:

To create a custom shortcode, follow these steps:

Define the Shortcode Function: In your theme's functions.php file or a custom plugin, define a function that generates the content for your shortcode. For example:

```
function custom_shortcode_function() {
    return "This is a custom shortcode content.";
}
```

Register the Shortcode: Use the add_shortcode function to register your shortcode and link it to your function. For example:

```
add_shortcode('custom_shortcode', 'custom_shortcode_function');
```

Use the Shortcode: In your post or page content, use your shortcode like this:

```
[custom_shortcode]
```

When the post or page is viewed on the front end, WordPress will replace [custom_shortcode] with the content generated by your custom_shortcode_function.

Implementing Shortcode Attributes: Shortcode attributes allow users to customize the behavior or appearance of a shortcode. To implement shortcode attributes, modify your shortcode function to accept an $atts parameter. For example:

```
function custom_shortcode_function($atts) {
    // Extract attributes with default values
    $atts = shortcode_atts(array(
        'attribute1' => 'default_value1',
        'attribute2' => 'default_value2',
    ), $atts);

    // Use attributes in shortcode content
    $content = "Attribute 1: {$atts['attribute1']}, Attribute 2: {$atts['attribute2']}";
    return $content;
}
```

Now, users can use your shortcode with attributes like this:

```
[custom_shortcode attribute1="value1" attribute2="value2"]
```

This allows for greater flexibility and customization when using your custom shortcode.

By understanding widgets, creating custom widgets, building shortcodes, and implementing shortcode attributes, you can enhance the functionality and customization options of your WordPress website, making it more dynamic and user-friendly.

Chapter 30: Working with the REST API

A decoupled WordPress application offers greater flexibility, scalability, and the ability to create highly customized user experiences. It's especially useful when you want to build interactive, dynamic web applications while still leveraging the content management capabilities of WordPress.

Introduction to the WordPress REST API: The WordPress REST API is a powerful feature that allows you to interact with your WordPress site's content and data using standard HTTP requests. It exposes your site's data in a structured, machine-readable format, making it accessible to other applications, websites, or services. Here's an overview of the WordPress REST API:

RESTful Principles: The API follows the principles of Representational State Transfer (REST), using HTTP methods like GET, POST, PUT, and DELETE to perform CRUD (Create, Read, Update, Delete) operations on resources.

JSON Format: Data is typically exchanged in JSON (JavaScript Object Notation) format, making it easy to work with in various programming languages.

Authentication: The API supports authentication mechanisms, allowing secure access to protected data. Common authentication methods include OAuth 1.0a, OAuth 2.0, and API keys.

Endpoints: WordPress provides a set of built-in API endpoints for common resources like posts, pages, users, and comments. Custom post types and taxonomies can also have their endpoints.

Creating and Consuming API Endpoints: You can create custom API endpoints in WordPress to expose specific data or functionality. Here's an overview of how to create and consume API endpoints:

Creating Custom API Endpoints: Define the Route: Use WordPress hooks like rest_api_init to define a custom API route.

You specify the URL path, the HTTP methods to allow, and the callback function that handles the request.

Implement the Callback Function: In your callback function, you retrieve and process data from your WordPress site. You can use standard WordPress functions to fetch data and format it as JSON.

Register the Endpoint: Use the register_rest_route function to register your custom endpoint.

Consuming API Endpoints: You can consume WordPress REST API endpoints from various clients, including web applications, mobile apps, or even external services. Here's how to do it:

Make HTTP Requests: Use standard HTTP client libraries or functions in your programming language of choice to make GET, POST, PUT, or DELETE requests to the API endpoints.

Parse JSON Responses: When you receive responses from the API, parse the JSON data to access the information you need.

Authentication: If your API requires authentication, include the necessary credentials or tokens in your requests.

Building a Decoupled WordPress Application: A decoupled WordPress application refers to a setup where the frontend (the part that users interact with) is separated from the backend (the WordPress content management system). In such a setup, the frontend can be built using different technologies, like JavaScript frameworks (e.g., React, Vue.js), while WordPress serves as a headless CMS.

Here are the steps to build a decoupled WordPress application:

Frontend Development: Choose a frontend technology or framework, such as React or Vue.js.

Set up your frontend project and define the user interface (UI) components.

WordPress as a Headless CMS: Expose the content and data you need via custom API endpoints, as mentioned earlier.

Ensure that your WordPress site has the necessary authentication mechanisms for secure access.

API Integration: In your frontend application, make HTTP requests to the WordPress REST API endpoints to fetch and display content.

Routing and Navigation: Implement routing and navigation in your frontend application to display different pages or views.

User Authentication: If your WordPress site requires user authentication, handle user logins and registrations within your frontend application, or integrate with WordPress's authentication endpoints.

Optimize for Performance: Consider using caching mechanisms and optimizing API requests to ensure fast performance.

Testing and Deployment: Thoroughly test your decoupled application for functionality and performance.

Deploy your frontend and backend separately, and ensure they can communicate over the internet.

Chapter 31: Ongoing Maintenance and Scaling

Regular Site Maintenance Tasks: Regular site maintenance is crucial to ensure that your WordPress website runs smoothly, remains secure, and provides a positive user experience. Here are some essential maintenance tasks:

WordPress Updates: Keep WordPress core, themes, and plugins updated to the latest versions. Updates often include security patches and bug fixes.

Security Audits: Regularly review user accounts and access permissions. Remove any unused or suspicious accounts.

Monitor for security vulnerabilities and consider using security plugins.

Implement strong passwords and two-factor authentication for user accounts.

Backup Your Website: Perform regular backups of your website's files and database. Store backups securely offsite.

Performance Optimization: Monitor website speed and performance. Optimize images, use caching plugins, and implement content delivery networks (CDNs) to improve load times.

Broken Links and 404 Errors: Periodically scan your site for broken links and correct them. Use tools or plugins to automate this process.

Database Cleanup: Optimize and clean up your WordPress database to improve efficiency. Consider using plugins for this purpose.

Spam Management: Monitor and manage comments and contact form submissions to prevent spam.

Content Review: Review and update outdated content, including posts, pages, and media files.

Regular Testing: Test your website across different browsers and devices to ensure it displays correctly.

Site Monitoring: Use website monitoring tools to receive alerts if your site experiences downtime or performance issues.

Scaling WordPress for High Traffic: Scaling your WordPress site for high traffic is essential to maintain performance and reliability. Here are strategies for scaling:

Caching: Implement caching solutions like W3 Total Cache or WP Super Cache to reduce server load and speed up page loading times.

Content Delivery Network (CDN): Use a CDN to distribute static assets (images, CSS, JavaScript) globally, reducing server load and improving load times for visitors worldwide.

Load Balancing: Set up load balancing to distribute incoming traffic across multiple servers, ensuring high availability and redundancy.

Database Optimization: Optimize your database for high traffic by using database caching and indexing.

Content Delivery: Consider offloading media content to external services like Amazon S3 or a content delivery network (CDN).

Managed Hosting: Choose a managed WordPress hosting provider that specializes in handling high-traffic websites. They often offer scalable solutions.

Content Caching: Cache dynamic content using object caching solutions like Redis or Memcached.

Content Delivery: Use a reverse proxy server like Nginx or Varnish to cache and serve static content.

Backup and Disaster Recovery Strategies: Protecting your website's data and having a disaster recovery plan in place is critical. Here's how to implement backup and recovery strategies:

Regular Backups: Schedule regular backups of your website's files and database. Automate this process using backup plugins or hosting provider features.

Offsite Storage: Store backups securely in an offsite location, such as cloud storage or a remote server.

Incremental Backups: Consider incremental backups to reduce storage space and backup duration. Only back up changes made since the last backup.

Disaster Recovery Plan: Develop a disaster recovery plan that outlines steps to restore your website in case of data loss or system failure.

Testing Backups: Periodically test your backups by restoring them to ensure they are functional.

Version Control: Use version control systems like Git to track changes to your site's code, making it easier to roll back to previous states if needed.

Security Measures: Implement strong security measures to prevent data breaches and unauthorized access to your backups.

Documentation: Document your backup and recovery procedures so that your team can follow them effectively during emergencies.

By regularly maintaining your WordPress site, implementing scaling strategies for high traffic, and having a robust backup and disaster recovery plan in place, you can ensure the security, performance, and reliability of your website, even in challenging situations.

Chapter 32: Performance Optimization

Improving the performance of your WordPress website is crucial for providing a fast and responsive user experience. Here are some performance best practices and caching strategies to reduce page load times:

Performance Best Practices:

Optimize Images: Use image optimization plugins or tools to compress images without sacrificing quality.

Specify image dimensions in HTML to prevent layout shifts as images load.

Use a Content Delivery Network (CDN): A CDN distributes your website's static assets (images, CSS, JavaScript) across multiple servers globally, reducing latency for users worldwide.

Minify CSS and JavaScript: Minify your CSS and JavaScript files to reduce their size by removing whitespace and unnecessary characters.

Combine multiple CSS and JavaScript files into fewer files to reduce HTTP requests.

Leverage Browser Caching: Set expiration headers for static resources to instruct browsers to cache them locally, reducing server requests for subsequent visits.

Enable GZIP Compression: Configure your server to compress content using GZIP or Brotli to reduce file sizes transmitted over the network.

Use Lazy Loading: Implement lazy loading for images and videos to defer their loading until they are in the user's viewport.

Minimize HTTP Requests: Reduce the number of HTTP requests by using CSS sprites for icons, combining CSS and JavaScript files, and limiting the use of external scripts.

Optimize Database Queries: Optimize database queries to reduce query execution time.

Use a caching mechanism for database queries, such as object caching with Redis or Memcached.

Utilize Browser Rendering: Prioritize above-the-fold content to load quickly, allowing users to see and interact with the page while other assets load in the background.

Choose a Fast-Hosting Provider: Select a reputable hosting provider with performance-optimized servers and server-level caching.

Caching Strategies for WordPress:

Page Caching: Use a page caching plugin like W3 Total Cache or WP Super Cache to generate and serve static HTML versions of your pages to reduce server load and improve load times.

Object Caching: Implement object caching with Redis or Memcached to store frequently accessed data in memory, reducing database queries.

Browser Caching: Enable browser caching by configuring your server to set appropriate cache headers for static resources.

Content Delivery Network (CDN): Pair a CDN with your caching strategy to cache and serve static assets from geographically distributed servers.

Reducing Page Load Times:

Optimize Critical Rendering Path: Prioritize loading critical resources (e.g., CSS for above-the-fold content) to ensure a faster initial page render.

Minimize Redirects: Reduce the use of redirects as each one adds an extra round-trip request, slowing down page load times.

Pre-connect and Prefetch: Use the <link rel="preconnect"> and <link rel="prefetch"> HTML tags to establish early connections to third-party domains and fetch critical resources in the background.

HTTP/2 and HTTP/3: Ensure your server supports the latest HTTP protocols, such as HTTP/2 and HTTP/3, which can significantly improve page load times by multiplexing requests.

Optimize Third-Party Scripts: Evaluate and limit the use of third-party scripts and services that can add latency to your site.

Monitor Performance: Regularly monitor your website's performance using tools like Google Page Speed Insights, GTmetrix, or WebPageTest to identify and address performance bottlenecks.

Content Delivery Optimization: Optimize content delivery by using a reliable hosting provider, leveraging CDNs, and choosing server locations that are geographically closer to your target audience.

Mobile Optimization: Ensure that your website is mobile-friendly and loads quickly on mobile devices.

By following these best practices and caching strategies, you can significantly reduce page load times, improve site performance, and enhance the user experience on your WordPress website.

Chapter 33: Advanced Theme Development

Customizing Theme Options Using the Customizer: The WordPress Customizer is a user-friendly interface that allows you to make various theme-related customizations and preview them in real-time. To customize theme options using the Customizer, follow these steps:

Access the Customizer: In your WordPress dashboard, go to "Appearance" > "Customize."

Select a Section: The Customizer typically displays a list of sections on the left-hand side. Click on the section you want to customize (e.g., Site Identity, Colors, Background Image, etc.).

Make Customizations: Depending on the section, you can modify various theme options. For example, in the "Site Identity" section, you can upload a site logo or change the site title and tagline.

Adjust settings such as colours, fonts, and header/footer layouts in their respective sections.

Live Preview: As you make changes, the live preview on the right-hand side will update in real-time, showing you how your site will look with the new customizations.

Save Changes: When you're satisfied with your customizations, click the "Publish" or "Save & Publish" button to make the changes live on your site.

Exit the Customizer: Click the "X" button at the top-left corner of the Customizer to exit and return to the WordPress dashboard.

Creating Custom Page Templates: Custom page templates in WordPress allow you to define unique layouts and functionalities for specific pages. Here's how to create a custom page template:

Create a New Template File: In your theme's directory, create a new PHP file and name it something descriptive (e.g., custom-template.php).

Define the Template Name: At the top of your template file, add the following comment to specify the template's name. This is how WordPress identifies it:

```
/*
Template Name: Custom Template
*/
```

Build the Template: Within the file, code the custom layout and functionality for your page.

You can include standard WordPress functions and template tags to display content dynamically.

Upload to Your Theme: Save the template file and upload it to your theme's directory.

Assign the Template to a Page: In the WordPress dashboard, create or edit a page where you want to use the custom template.

In the Page Attributes section, you should see a Template dropdown. Select your custom template from the list.

Publish or Update the Page: Publish the page or update it if you're editing an existing one.

View the Page: When you view the page on the front end, it will use your custom template's layout and functionality.

Implementing Theme Customization Best Practices: When customizing themes and creating custom templates, consider the following best practices:

Use Child Themes: If you're making significant customizations to a theme, create a child theme to preserve your changes when the parent theme is updated.

Document Your Customizations: Keep a record of your customizations, including code changes and theme settings, for future reference.

Test Responsiveness: Ensure that your customizations maintain a responsive design and work well on various screen sizes.

Follow WordPress Coding Standards: Adhere to WordPress coding standards to ensure clean and maintainable code.

Backup Your Site: Before making extensive theme customizations, always back up your website to avoid data loss.

Optimize for Performance: Test the performance impact of your customizations and optimize code and assets for speed.

Consider Accessibility: Ensure that your customizations follow accessibility best practices to make your site usable for all visitors.

By customizing theme options using the Customizer, creating custom page templates, and following best practices, you can tailor your WordPress website to meet your design and functionality needs while maintaining code quality and performance.

www.ingramcontent.com/pod-product-compliance
Lightning Source LLC
La Vergne TN
LVHW051538050326
832903LV00033B/4311

9798860096738